THE OFFICIAL SOUTHAMPTON FOOTBALL CLUB ANNUAL 2021

WRITTEN BY MARK PERROW & TOM HARVEY
DESIGNED BY JON DALRYMPLE

A Grange Publication

© 2020. Published by Grange Communications Ltd., Edinburgh, under licence from Southampton Football Club. Printed in the EU.

Every effort has been made to ensure the accuracy of information within this publication but the publishers cannot be held responsible for any errors or omissions. Views expressed are those of the author and do not necessarily represent those of the publishers or the football club. All rights reserved.

Photographs © Southampton FC / Getty Images / Reuters

ISBN 978-1-913578-04-6

CONTENTS

WELCOME	5
SEASON REVIEW	6
QUIZ OF THE SEASON	24
PLAYER AWARDS	26
KING INGS	28
EAT LIKE A SAINT	33
SEASON IN NUMBERS	34
BEHIND THE SCENES	36
LOCKDOWN QUIZ	39
MEET THE NEXT GENERATION	40
SOUTHAMPTON FC WOMEN	42
BEST OF THE SAINTS	44
CULT HERO: GULY DO PRADO	46
PICK YOUR CULT HERO XI	47
WORD PUZZLES	48
DRINK LIKE A SAINT	49
GETTING TO KNOW: KYLE WALKER-PETERS	50
2020/21 KIT	52
PRE-SEASON	54
MEET THE OPPOSITION	56
THANK YOU!	60
QUIZ & PUZZLE ANSWERS	62

WELCOME

TO THE OFFICIAL SOUTHAMPTON FOOTBALL CLUB ANNUAL 2021!

What a year 2020 has been. Like every other industry, football has been hit by the COVID-19 pandemic, and only with the unwavering support of the Saints family have we been able to tackle this significant challenge together.

Off the field, we have reached out to our local community and tried to help those in need, whilst the exceptional loyalty and goodwill of our fans has supported us through unprecedented times.

On the field, after the 2019/20 Premier League campaign came to an abrupt halt, the players and staff regrouped, led by our inspirational manager, to produce some of their best football of the season after the restart.

Ultimately, this book remains a celebration of all the on-pitch highs from 2019/20, featuring the full story of this unique season; the demolition derby at Fratton Park, the festive renaissance that saw Saints win four Premier League away games in a row, and the blistering post-lockdown form that saw Ralph Hasenhüttl's men topple reigning champions Manchester City.

There is a special section dedicated to Danny Ings's spectacular goalscoring exploits, as the striker became the first Saint to hit 20 in a top-flight campaign since James Beattie in 2002/03, along with a host of quizzes and games to test your knowledge of all things Southampton.

Elsewhere, we turn back the clock by getting to know some club legends and cult heroes, whilst introducing summer signing Kyle Walker-Peters and Academy starlets Will Smallbone and Jake Vokins to get you excited about the future.

Enjoy your read!

SEASON REVIEW 2019/20
AUGUST

The new campaign began in disappointing fashion as Saints conceded three times in the final 27 minutes to leave Burnley empty-handed.

Liverpool represented the first home fixture of the season and goals from Sadio Mané and Roberto Firmino put the visitors in command, as Danny Ings's late effort against his former side proved no more than a consolation.

Saints recorded their first victory of the season at Brighton. The Seagulls saw Florin Andone dismissed, before substitute Moussa Djenepo opened his Southampton account. Nathan Redmond sealed the points in injury time.

Southampton travelled to the capital for a Carabao Cup second-round tie at Championship Fulham and came through unscathed thanks to Michael Obafemi's second-half winner.

The month concluded with a point at home to Manchester United. The Red Devils led early on, but Saints levelled through Jannik Vestergaard's header. Kevin Danso was sent off with 17 minutes left, but United couldn't find a way past an inspired Angus Gunn.

MOMENT OF THE MONTH
Moussa Djenepo arrives off the bench at Brighton to score his first Saints goal, helping his new club to their first win of the season.

BURNLEY 3-0 SAINTS

SAINTS 1-2 LIVERPOOL

FULHAM 0-1 SAINTS

SAINTS 1-1 MAN UTD

BRIGHTON 0-2 SAINTS

RESULTS

Burnley	3-0	Saints	L
Saints	1-2	Liverpool	L
Brighton	0-2	Saints	W
Fulham	0-1	Saints	W *
Saints	1-1	Man Utd	D

*Carabao Cup R2

HOW IT STOOD

		Pld	GD	Pts
11.	Burnley	4	-1	4
12.	Everton	3	-1	4
13.	SAINTS	4	-2	4
14.	Newcastle	4	-2	4
15.	Bournemouth	4	-3	4

SEASON REVIEW 2019/20
SEPTEMBER

Saints' upturn in form continued with victory at Premier League newcomers Sheffield United. Moussa Djenepo scored a spectacular solo winner in the second half, while the Blades had Billy Sharp sent off with five minutes left.

A frustrating Friday night home loss to Bournemouth followed. Saints trailed 2-0 at the break, but James Ward-Prowse's penalty gave the hosts hope until Callum Wilson wrapped up the win.

Saints were much improved when they thumped Portsmouth in the third round of the Carabao Cup at Fratton Park. In the first south coast derby for seven years, Danny Ings scored twice in the opening 45 minutes before Cédric and Nathan Redmond got in on the act on a night to remember for the travelling fans.

A run of four straight away wins was halted on the club's first visit to the Tottenham Hotspur Stadium. Tanguy Ndombele put Spurs in front, before Serge Aurier was sent off. Ings levelled, but Harry Kane scored the winner just before half time.

MOMENT OF THE MONTH
Boyhood Southampton fan Danny Ings celebrates in front of the Portsmouth supporters after scoring in the 4-0 win at Fratton Park.

SHEFFIELD UTD 0-1 SAINTS

SAINTS 1-3 BOURNEMOUTH

PORTSMOUTH 0-4 SAINTS

SPURS 2-1 SAINTS

RESULTS

Sheffield Utd	0-1	Saints	W
Saints	1-3	Bournemouth	L
Portsmouth	0-4	Saints	W *
Spurs	2-1	Saints	L

*Carabao Cup R3

HOW IT STOOD

		Pld	GD	Pts
12.	Sheffield Utd	7	0	8
13.	Wolves	7	-2	7
14.	SAINTS	7	-4	7
15.	Everton	7	-6	7
16.	Brighton	7	-5	6

SEASON REVIEW 2019/20
OCTOBER

Danny Ings was again on target, but it counted for little as Saints were beaten at home by Chelsea to slip to a third successive league defeat.

The striker found the net once more to put Southampton in front at Wolves – his fourth goal in consecutive games – but Raúl Jiménez's penalty ensured the spoils were shared.

The least said about the next game the better – a 9-0 loss at the hands of Leicester at a rainswept St Mary's. Saints had Ryan Bertrand dismissed by VAR for an incident in the build-up to the opener and the Foxes took advantage as the depleted hosts suffered their biggest-ever league defeat.

It didn't get any easier with a trip to Manchester City in the fourth round of the Carabao Cup. The visitors were 3-0 down before Jack Stephens pulled one back with a quarter of an hour remaining as Saints exited the competition.

MOMENT OF THE MONTH
Danny Ings slides on his knees in front of the travelling Saints fans in familiar fashion after breaking the deadlock at Wolves.

SAINTS 1-4 CHELSEA

WOLVES 1-1 SAINTS

SAINTS 0-9 LEICESTER

MAN CITY 3-1 SAINTS

RESULTS

Saints	1-4	Chelsea	L
Wolves	1-1	Saints	D
Man City	3-1	Saints	L*
Saints	0-9	Leicester	L

*Carabao Cup R4

HOW IT STOOD

		Pld	GD	Pts
16.	Everton	10	-6	10
17.	Newcastle	10	-9	9
18.	SAINTS	10	-16	8
19.	Norwich	10	-13	7
20.	Watford	10	-16	5

SEASON REVIEW 2019/20
NOVEMBER

Saints were back at the Etihad just a few days later in the Premier League and things were looking up when James Ward-Prowse scored. Southampton held out until Sergio Agüero levelled with 20 minutes to go, before Kyle Walker hit a gut-wrenching late winner.

Back at home, an early goal put Everton in front at St Mary's, but Danny Ings equalised in the 50th minute only for Richarlison to win it for the Toffees.

Saints were then seconds away from a memorable victory at Arsenal, deservedly leading twice through Ings and Ward-Prowse, before Alexandre Lacazette scored in the sixth minute of injury time to salvage a point for the Gunners.

A run of eight league games without victory ended when Watford were beaten at St Mary's. The Hornets led through Ismaïla Sarr but Ings restored parity on 78 minutes and Ward-Prowse curled home a beauty of a free-kick soon after to win it in dramatic fashion.

MOMENT OF THE MONTH
Cometh the hour, cometh the man: James Ward-Prowse hits the jackpot with a late free-kick to overcome Watford at St Mary's.

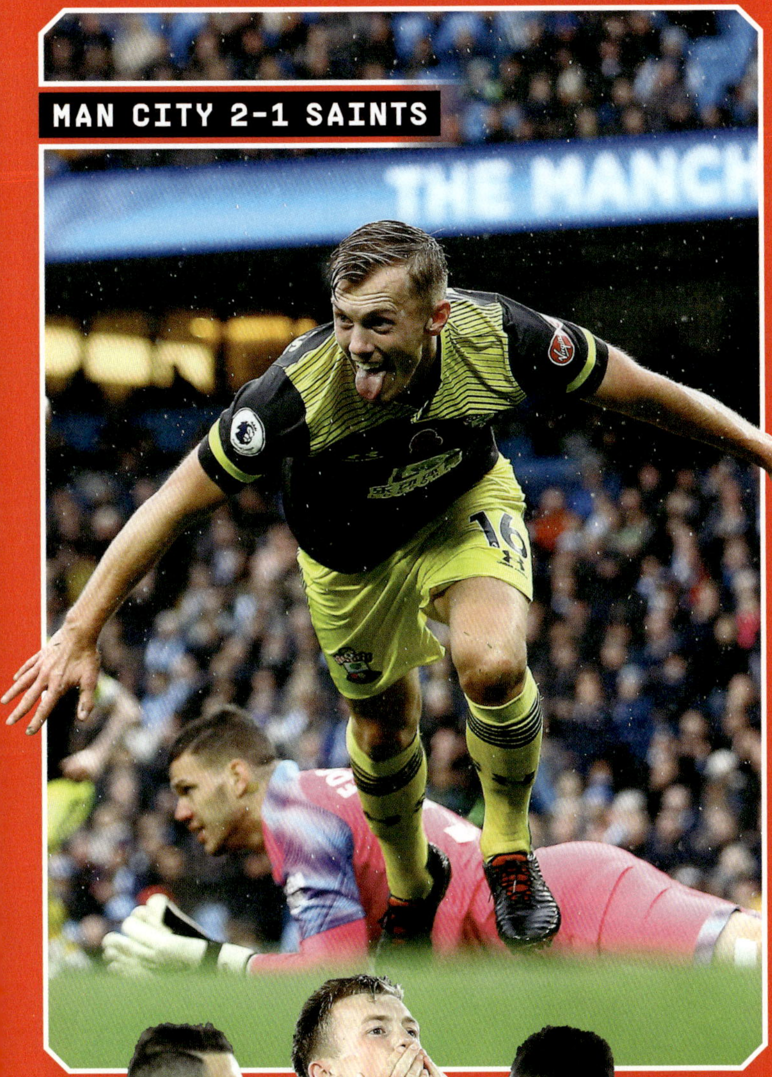

MAN CITY 2-1 SAINTS

SAINTS 1-2 EVERTON

ARSENAL 2-2 SAINTS

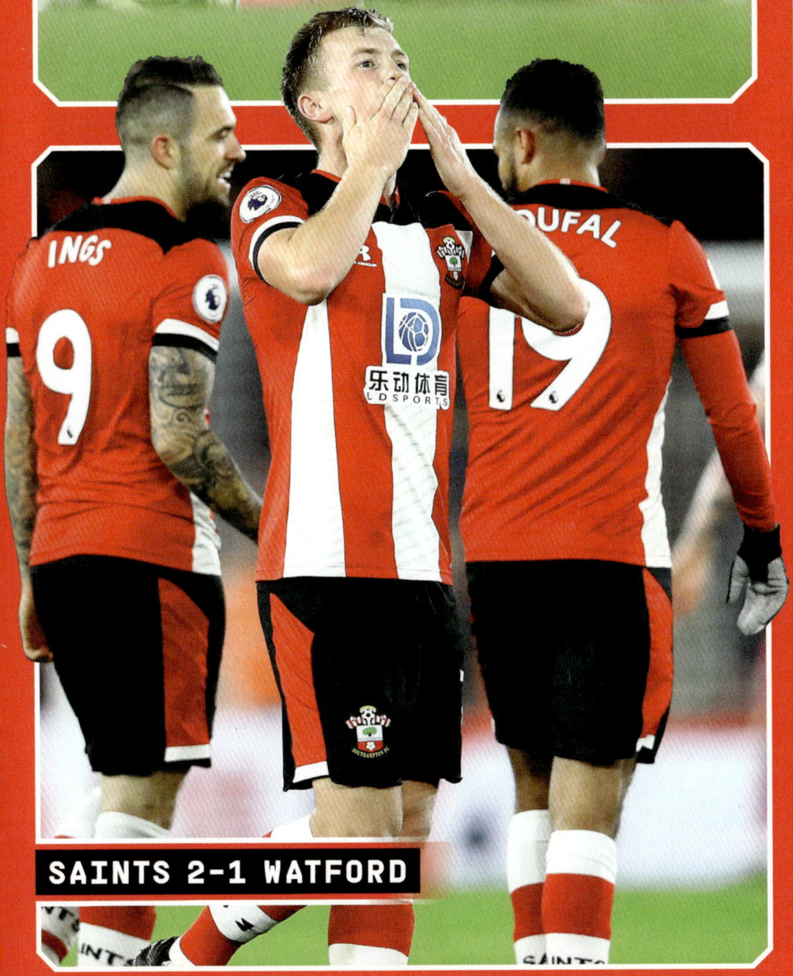

SAINTS 2-1 WATFORD

RESULTS

Man City	2-1	Saints	L
Saints	1-2	Everton	L
Arsenal	2-2	Saints	D
Saints	2-1	Watford	W

HOW IT STOOD

		Pld	GD	Pts
16.	Aston Villa	14	-1	14
17.	Everton	13	-7	14
18.	SAINTS	14	-17	12
19.	Norwich	13	-15	10
20.	Watford	14	-19	8

SEASON REVIEW 2019/20
DECEMBER

Ralph Hasenhüttl celebrated a year in charge with victory at home to Norwich. Danny Ings headed the hosts in front and Ryan Bertrand doubled the advantage, before Teemu Pukki registered for City.

Ings scored for the fifth game in a row to put Southampton in the lead at Newcastle but Jonjo Shelvey equalised and Federico Fernández bagged a late winner for the Magpies.

West Ham left St Mary's with three points thanks to Sébastien Haller's first-half effort, but Ings was on the money again just before Christmas, scoring twice either side of a Jack Stephens header in a welcome win at Aston Villa. Jack Grealish pulled one back for the hosts.

Boxing Day provided more Christmas cheer as Chelsea were defeated at Stamford Bridge thanks to fine goals from Michael Obafemi and Nathan Redmond.

Ings bagged his 14th of the campaign to cancel out James Tomkins's opener as Southampton's final game of 2019 ended in a draw with Crystal Palace.

MOMENT OF THE MONTH
Nathan Redmond leaps to the heavens after rounding off a superb team move to double Saints' lead at Chelsea on Boxing Day.

SAINTS 2-1 NORWICH

CHELSEA 0-2 SAINTS

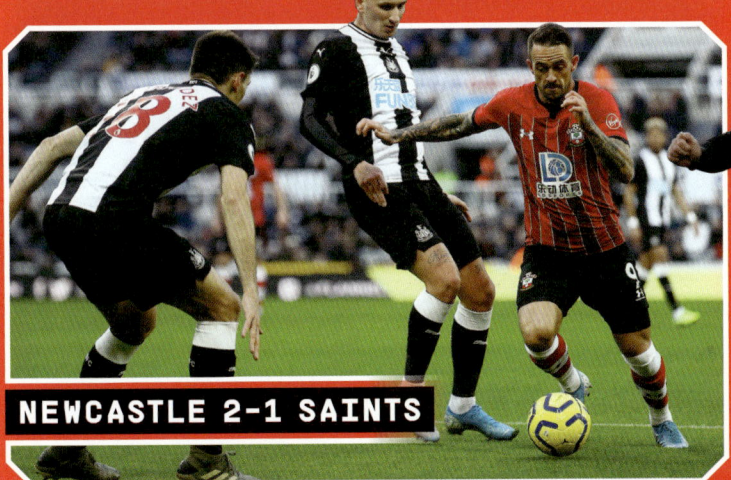
NEWCASTLE 2-1 SAINTS

SAINTS 1-1 CRYSTAL PALACE

SAINTS 0-1 WEST HAM

ASTON VILLA 1-3 SAINTS

RESULTS

Saints	2-1	Norwich	W
Newcastle	2-1	Saints	L
Saints	0-1	West Ham	L
Aston Villa	1-3	Saints	W
Chelsea	0-2	Saints	W
Saints	1-1	Crystal Palace	D

HOW IT STOOD

		Pld	GD	Pts
13.	Burnley	20	-9	24
14.	Brighton	20	-4	23
15.	SAINTS	20	-14	22
16.	Bournemouth	20	-8	20
17.	West Ham	19	-11	19

SEASON REVIEW 2019/20
JANUARY

The resurgence continued as a brilliant Danny Ings goal defeated Tottenham at St Mary's on New Year's Day.

Will Smallbone scored on his debut and fellow Academy graduate Jake Vokins also found the net on his first start as Saints beat Championship side Huddersfield in the FA Cup third round at St Mary's.

Southampton made amends for the Leicester result in October by beating the Foxes on their own turf. Dennis Praet tapped City in front, but Stuart Armstrong quickly equalised and Ings won it with nine minutes left.

The unbeaten run ended as Saints let a 2-0 half-time lead slip to lose to Wolves at St Mary's. Jan Bednarek and Shane Long were on target for Southampton.

Saints recovered to win at Crystal Palace as superb goals from Nathan Redmond and Armstrong earned a fourth successive away victory. Sofiane Boufal's late equaliser secured a deserved replay after a 1-1 draw at home to Tottenham in the fourth round of the FA Cup.

MOMENT OF THE MONTH
Saints' festive resurgence continues into the new year with an emotional victory at Leicester, burying some demons along the way.

SAINTS 1-0 SPURS

SAINTS 2-0 HUDDERSFIELD

LEICESTER 1-2 SAINTS

CRYSTAL PALACE 0-2 SAINTS

SAINTS 2-3 WOLVES

SAINTS 1-1 SPURS

RESULTS

Saints	1-0	Spurs	W
Saints	2-0	Huddersfield	W *
Leicester	1-2	Saints	W
Saints	2-3	Wolves	L
Crystal Palace	0-2	Saints	W
Saints	1-1	Spurs	D **

*FA Cup R3   **FA Cup R4

HOW IT STOOD

		Pld	GD	Pts
7.	Wolves	24	3	34
8.	Sheffield Utd	24	2	33
9.	SAINTS	24	2	31
10.	Arsenal	24	-2	30
11.	Crystal Palace	24	-6	30

SEASON REVIEW 2019/20

FEBRUARY / MARCH

Southampton's fine away form was ended by runaway league leaders Liverpool at Anfield, before an 87th-minute penalty sent Saints out of the FA Cup in a fourth-round replay at Spurs, despite Shane Long and Danny Ings firing the visitors in front.

Ings was on target again at St Mary's but Saints were beaten by Burnley in wet and windy conditions brought on by Storm Dennis.

However, Southampton returned to winning ways with victory over struggling Aston Villa. Long scored early on and Stuart Armstrong made sure of the win in stoppage time.

Southampton were beaten by West Ham at the London Stadium. Michael Obafemi cancelled out Jarrod Bowen's opener, but Sébastien Haller and former Saint Michael Antonio sealed victory for the Hammers.

Saints' last game before football came to a halt due to the coronavirus pandemic was at home to Newcastle, where a late goal from Allan Saint-Maximin won it for the Toon after Moussa Djenepo was sent off and Alex McCarthy saved a penalty.

MOMENT OF THE MONTH
Stuart Armstrong races towards the Saints fans after wrapping up three vital points with a late clincher against Aston Villa.

LIVERPOOL 4-0 SAINTS

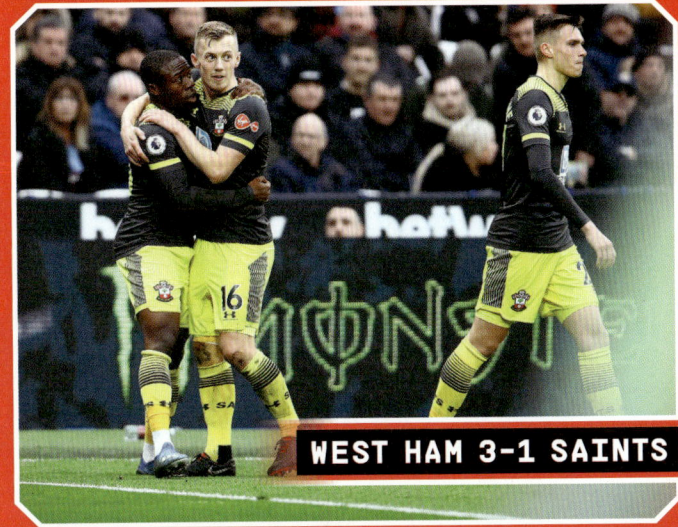
WEST HAM 3-1 SAINTS

SPURS 3-2 SAINTS

SAINTS 0-1 NEWCASTLE

SAINTS 1-2 BURNLEY

SAINTS 2-0 ASTON VILLA

RESULTS

Liverpool	4-0	Saints	L
Spurs	3-2	Saints	L *
Saints	1-2	Burnley	L
Saints	2-0	Aston Villa	W
West Ham	3-1	Saints	L
Saints	0-1	Newcastle	L

*FA Cup R4 Replay

HOW IT STOOD

		Pld	GD	Pts
12.	Everton	29	-9	37
13.	Newcastle	29	-16	35
14.	SAINTS	29	-16	34
15.	Brighton	29	-8	29
16.	West Ham	29	-15	27

SEASON REVIEW 2019/20
JUNE

When football resumed 104 days later, fans weren't allowed into stadiums, but Southampton made light work of Norwich at an empty Carrow Road.

Danny Ings curled in the opener shortly after half time, before Stuart Armstrong doubled the lead five minutes later. Nathan Redmond scored the third against his old club late on.

Saints suffered their final loss of the season when they were beaten by Arsenal at St Mary's. Eddie Nketiah put the Gunners in front and when Jack Stephens was sent off with five minutes left, the resulting free-kick fell the way of Joe Willock to make sure of victory.

The club's fine form on the road continued with an impressive win at relegation-threatened Watford. Two goals from Ings had Saints in the ascendency, but Jan Bednarek put through his own net before James Ward-Prowse's sumptuous free-kick settled the contest, paving the way for an impressive end to the campaign for Ralph Hasenhüttl's rejuvenated team.

MOMENT OF THE MONTH
Danny Ings celebrates reaching 20 goals in all competitions with a brace at Watford, firing Saints to the much-coveted 40-point mark.

NORWICH 0-3 SAINTS

SAINTS 0-2 ARSENAL

WATFORD 1-3 SAINTS

RESULTS

Norwich	0-3	Saints	W
Saints	0-2	Arsenal	L
Watford	1-3	Saints	W

HOW IT STOOD

		Pld	GD	Pts
11.	Crystal Palace	32	-9	42
12.	Everton	31	-8	41
13.	SAINTS	32	-14	40
14.	Newcastle	31	-13	39
15.	Brighton	32	-10	33

SEASON REVIEW 2019/20
JULY

Ché Adams's first Saints goal – a 40-yard lob – secured victory over Manchester City in spectacular fashion at St Mary's.

Danny Ings put Saints in front after James Ward-Prowse's missed penalty at Everton, for whom Richarlison equalised against the run of play.

Michael Obafemi's 96th-minute equaliser saw Saints snatch a point at Manchester United. Stuart Armstrong opened the scoring, but quick-fire goals from United turned the game on its head, until substitute Obafemi pounced at the death.

Ings became the first Saints player to score 20 Premier League goals in a season since James Beattie with a 66th-minute equaliser at home to Brighton, before firing Saints in front at relegation-threatened Bournemouth. He later saw a penalty saved, but Adams sealed victory in added time.

Southampton came from behind on the final day to defeat Sheffield United at St Mary's and ensure an unbeaten July. Adams continued his purple patch with a brace against his old side before Ings won and converted a late spot-kick.

MOMENT OF THE MONTH
Ché Adams is mobbed by his teammates after finally scoring his first Saints goal – doing so in unforgettable style against Man City.

SAINTS 1-0 MAN CITY

EVERTON 1-1 SAINTS

MAN UTD 2-2 SAINTS

SAINTS 1-1 BRIGHTON

BOURNEMOUTH 0-2 SAINTS

SAINTS 3-1 SHEFFIELD UTD

RESULTS

Saints	1-0	Man City	W
Everton	1-1	Saints	D
Man Utd	2-2	Saints	D
Saints	1-1	Brighton	D
Bournemouth	0-2	Saints	W
Saints	3-1	Sheffield Utd	W

HOW IT STOOD

		Pld	GD	Pts
1.	Liverpool (C)	38	+52	99
2.	Man City	38	+67	81
3.	Man Utd	38	+30	66
4.	Chelsea	38	+15	66
5.	Leicester	38	+26	62
6.	Tottenham	38	+14	59
7.	Wolves	38	+11	59
8.	Arsenal	38	+8	56
9.	Sheffield Utd	38	0	54
10.	Burnley	38	-7	54
11.	SAINTS	38	-9	52
12.	Everton	38	-12	49
13.	Newcastle	38	-20	44
14.	Crystal Palace	38	-19	43
15.	Brighton	38	-15	41
16.	West Ham	38	-13	39
17.	Aston Villa	38	-26	35
18.	Bournemouth (R)	38	-25	34
19.	Watford (R)	38	-28	34
20.	Norwich (R)	38	-49	21

QUIZ OF THE

1. Saints signed Moussa Djenepo in the summer of 2019, but from which club?

2. Who did Saints record their first Premier League win of the season against?

3. Who scored the winner as Saints beat Fulham in the second round of the Carabao Cup?

4. Who scored the fourth goal against Portsmouth in the third round?

5. Danny Ings started a five-match scoring streak against Everton in November, but which team ended his run with a clean sheet at Saints' expense?

6. Saints won back-to-back home games 2-1 across November and December, but against which teams?

7. Saints beat Huddersfield in the FA Cup third round – which two players scored on their full debuts?

8. Saints went five Premier League games undefeated in December and January, with four wins. Who was the only team to deny Ralph Hasenhüttl's men victory?

9. Saints beat Crystal Palace 2-0 at Selhurst Park to put them in their highest Premier League placing of the season. What position was it?

10. Who scored a late equaliser to earn an FA Cup fourth round replay against Tottenham?

SEASON

11 Who was Saints' last win against before lockdown?

12 Which member of the squad received the most yellow cards in 2019/20?

13 Four players saw red during the season; who are they?

14 Who scored their first goal of the season after the Premier League restart?

15 Who were the only team to beat Saints after the restart?

16 How many shots did Saints face against Manchester City at St Mary's without conceding; 26, 29 or 32?

17 Who scored a last-gasp equaliser at Old Trafford to rescue a point?

18 How many consecutive penalties did Saints miss before Danny Ings scored from the spot on the final day of the campaign?

19 Saints kept their last clean sheet of the season against which team?

20 Who was the last player to score 20 Premier League goals in a season for Saints before Danny Ings?

2019/20 PLAYER AWARDS

MEN'S FIRST TEAM

Virgin Media Fans' Player of the Season
DANNY INGS

"I felt as soon as I came to Southampton that I had a great bond with the fans. It's great – thanks to everybody that did vote for me! It means a lot and gives me great hunger to improve and be better."

Monster Energy Players' Player of the Season
DANNY INGS

"It's nice to know you're doing everything you can for the team and the lads are noticing that. I can't thank them enough for everything they've done throughout the season to help me score the goals I have."

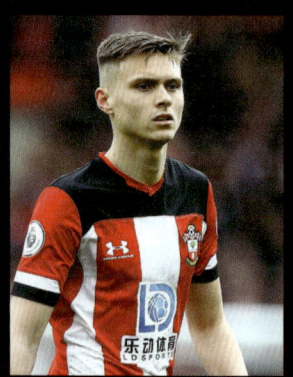

Utilita First Team Young Player of the Season
WILL SMALLBONE

Imperial Cars Goal of the Season
CHÉ ADAMS
vs Manchester City (H)

President's Choice Award
JAMES WARD-PROWSE

"The fact James played every minute in the Premier League speaks incredibly highly of him, and being made the captain just shows the respect that exists for him within the club." – Terry Paine, Honorary Club President

ACADEMY

Kuflink Scholar of the Year
ALEX JANKEWITZ

WOMEN'S FIRST TEAM

Fans' Player of the Season
ELLA MORRIS

Players' Player of the Season
ELLA MORRIS

"Ella had an impactful first season within the Women's squad, having stepped up from the RTC Under-16s. She has enormous potential and we look forward to her continuing to develop and grow with us." – Marieanne Spacey-Cale, Head of Girls' and Women's Football

Goal of the Season
RACHEL PANTING
vs Coventry United (H)

"I must admit I probably acted a bit like a kid after I scored, celebrating with my knee slide! But whatever your age, if you're someone who enjoys scoring, in an occasion like that, it's a natural reaction."

Southampton Way Award
RACHEL PANTING

WOMEN'S DEVELOPMENT SQUAD

Player of the Season JESS TANNER
Southampton Way Award KITTY CLEEVE

GIRLS' REGIONAL TALENT CLUB

Player of the Season ELLIE HEAD

KING INGS!

2019/20 was an outstanding individual campaign for DANNY INGS, scorer of a staggering 25 goals in all competitions – one of the most prolific seasons ever from a Saint! Here's how he did it…

1

LIVERPOOL (H)
17/08/19
Up and running against his former club, forcing Adrián into an embarrassing mistake.

PORTSMOUTH (A)
24/09/19
Picking his spot from the edge of the box after a clever turn outwits two defenders.

2

3

PORTSMOUTH (A)
24/09/19
Tells Michael Obafemi where he wants it, dinks the keeper, goads the locals. Lovely.

TOTTENHAM (A)
28/09/19
Another goalkeeper pressed into submission – this time Hugo Lloris is dispossessed.

4

5

CHELSEA (H)
06/10/19
A classic poacher's goal, darting across his man at the near post to convert a cross.

6. WOLVES (A)
19/10/19
A clever touch across the last defender, buying himself enough space to slot home.

7. EVERTON (H)
09/11/19
Right place, right time inside a crowded penalty area – it was becoming a happy habit.

8. ARSENAL (A)
23/11/19
Ryan Bertrand's quick thinking at a free-kick dispatched by a fine finish off the post.

9. WATFORD (H)
30/11/19
Smashed high into the net from close range after Moussa Djenepo's wing wizardry.

10. NORWICH (H)
04/12/19
A glancing header at the near post from a trademark James Ward-Prowse delivery.

11. NEWCASTLE (A)
08/12/19
Racing in behind the defence to score for a fifth consecutive Premier League game.

ASTON VILLA (A)
21/12/19
Beating ex-teammate Matt Targett to the loose ball from Shane Long's parried shot.

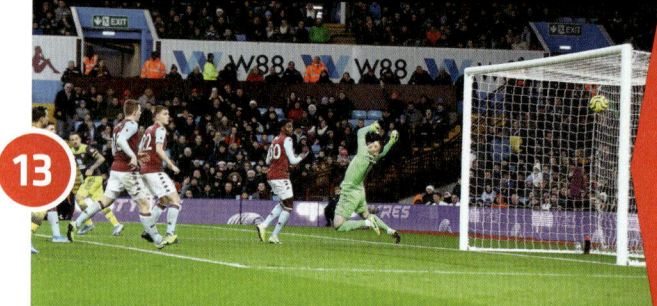

ASTON VILLA (A)
21/12/19
A deflected cross demands expert improvisation and a sharp left-footed finish.

CRYSTAL PALACE (H)
28/12/19
Anticipation is key: first to react to a sloppy backpass to finish 2019 on a high.

TOTTENHAM (H)
01/01/20
New year, same result, leaving former Saint Toby Alderweireld trailing in his wake.

LEICESTER (A)
11/01/20
An emotional victory secured by a late toe-poke through Kasper Schmeichel's legs.

TOTTENHAM (A)
05/02/20
Crowning a stunning counter-attack with a delightful curled finish in the FA Cup.

BURNLEY (H)
15/02/20

No mercy against his former club, beating Nick Pope with a precise 20-yard shot.

NORWICH (A)
19/06/20

Back in style after the restart, the whipped finish inside the far post is vintage Ings.

WATFORD (A)
28/06/20

Skipping away from his marker to buy himself time to take aim and find the corner.

WATFORD (A)
28/06/20

All his own work, with a little help from a wayward throw out by keeper Ben Foster.

EVERTON (A)
09/07/20

A career-high sixth goal against Everton, as his nifty footwork fools Jordan Pickford.

BRIGHTON (H)
16/07/20

The landmark 20th in the Prem, sliding home Nathan Redmond's threaded pass.

BOURNEMOUTH (A)
19/07/20
Back where he began, another keeper unsighted by a shot steered around a defender.

24

25

SHEFFIELD UNITED (H)
26/07/20
His only penalty, stroked past Dean Henderson, six minutes from the season's end.

MONTH BY MONTH

	Apps	Goals
Aug	5	1
Sep	4	3
Oct	3	2
Nov	4	3
Dec	6	5
Jan	5	2
Feb	5	2
Mar	1	0
Jun	3	3
Jul	6	4
TOTAL	42	25

ASSISTED BY...

Nathan Redmond	3
Stuart Armstrong	2
Jack Stephens	2
James Ward-Prowse	2
Ché Adams	1
Ryan Bertrand	1
Sofiane Boufal	1
Moussa Djenepo	1
Pierre-Emile Højbjerg	1
Shane Long	1
Michael Obafemi	1
Will Smallbone	1
Yan Valery	1

(Seven goals were not assisted by a teammate)

HOW HE SCORED THEM...

Right foot	16
Left foot	8
Header	1

WHERE HE SCORED THEM...

Inside six-yard box	7
Inside penalty area	13
Outside penalty area	5

PREMIER LEAGUE GOLDEN BOOT RACE 2019/20

Jamie Vardy	Leicester	23
Danny Ings	Saints	22
Pierre-Emerick Aubameyang	Arsenal	22
Raheem Sterling	Man City	20
Mohamed Salah	Liverpool	19
Sadio Mané	Liverpool	18
Harry Kane	Tottenham	18

SAINTS' MOST PROLIFIC TOP-FLIGHT SCORERS

1966/67	Ron Davies	37
1967/68	Ron Davies	28
1981/82	Kevin Keegan	26
1993/94	Matt Le Tissier	25
2002/03	James Beattie	23
1979/80	Phil Boyer	23
2019/20	Danny Ings	22

CHEF'S CORNER

Saints' Executive Head Chef, Zoltan Szalas, shares one of his favourite recipes for you to try out at home...

EAT LIKE A SAINT! SAINTS ENERGY BALLS

This is a little treat that is easy and fun to make. It is also one of the favoured takeaway snacks for the first-team after a match, and is great for providing a boost if you're on your bike or going for a run.

FACT: If you are following a vegan diet, you can swap the honey for maple syrup and the Nutella for a vegan peanut butter or vegan coco spread!

(For diabetic diets, please leave out the honey and Nutella)

Method
Servings: 48 balls/6 per portion

Ingredients
- 350g oats
- 200g Nutella or hazelnut spread
- 60g desiccated coconut
- 340g honey
- 150g roasted hazelnuts
- 4 tbsp ground flax seeds
- 2 tbsp chia seeds
- 4 tsp vanilla extract
- 1 tsp salt

Method
1. Put all the ingredients together in a food processor and pulse until combined. Cover the mixture and transfer to the fridge, and let cool for about 30-60 minutes. This will slightly harden the mixture and make it easier to form into balls.

2. Once mixture is cool, remove and roll into balls of your desired size.

3. To add some extra flavour, you can roll the balls in desiccated coconut, cocoa powder, crushed pistachios or crushed biscuits.

THE SEASON

44 — GAMES PLAYED BY JAMES WARD-PROWSE, SAINTS' ONLY EVER-PRESENT IN ALL COMPETITIONS

22 — PREMIER LEAGUE GOALS SCORED BY DANNY INGS – THE MOST BY A SAINT SINCE 2002/03

7 — ASSISTS BY NATHAN REDMOND, SAINTS' MOST PROLIFIC PROVIDER FOR THE SECOND SEASON RUNNING

18 — GAMES WON AND LOST BY SAINTS IN ALL COMPETITIONS – THERE WERE EIGHT DRAWS

16 — PL TEAMS DANNY INGS SCORED AGAINST – ONLY MAN CITY, MAN UTD AND WEST HAM KEPT HIM OUT

9 — THE NUMBER OF PREMIER LEAGUE AWAY GAMES WON BY SAINTS – A NEW CLUB RECORD

3,420 — MINUTES PLAYED BY JAMES WARD-PROWSE IN THE PL – THAT'S EVERY MINUTE OF EVERY GAME!

29,547 — SAINTS' AVERAGE HOME LEAGUE ATTENDANCE, PRIOR TO GAMES BEHIND CLOSED DOORS

1 — MANAGER OF THE MONTH AWARDS FOR RALPH HASENHÜTTL – HIS FIRST IN THE PL

128 — DANNY INGS AVERAGED ONE GOAL EVERY 128 MINUTES IN THE PREMIER LEAGUE

4 — RED CARDS FOR SAINTS PLAYERS IN THE PREMIER LEAGUE – ONLY ARSENAL (5) RECEIVED MORE

53 — YELLOW CARDS FOR SAINTS PLAYERS – ONLY LIVERPOOL AND LEICESTER RECEIVED LESS IN THE PL

499 — SHOTS ATTEMPTED BY SAINTS PLAYERS IN THE TOP FLIGHT, AT AN AVERAGE OF 13 PER GAME

16 — TIMES SAINTS HIT THE WOODWORK IN THE PL – ONLY MAN CITY AND LIVERPOOL DID SO MORE OFTEN

IN NUMBERS

15 — AWAY GOALS SCORED BY DANNY INGS IN ALL COMPETITIONS, 60% OF HIS SEASON TOTAL

29 — GAMES PLAYED BY CHÉ ADAMS WITHOUT SCORING, BEFORE NETTING FOUR GOALS IN SIX MATCHES

442.1 — KM RAN BY JAMES WARD-PROWSE – THE MOST OF ANY PL PLAYER, AVERAGING 11.63KM PER GAME

79 — SUCCESSFUL TAKE-ONS BY NATHAN REDMOND, THE FIFTH HIGHEST IN THE LEAGUE

12 — CLEAN SHEETS KEPT BY SAINTS IN ALL COMPETITIONS, INCLUDING 9 IN THE PREMIER LEAGUE

79 — SAVES MADE BY ALEX MCCARTHY IN 28 PL APPEARANCES; ANGUS GUNN MADE 30 IN 10

193 — CLEARANCES MADE BY JAN BEDNAREK – ONLY JAMES TARKOWSKI OF BURNLEY MADE MORE

103 — DAYS WITHOUT PLAYING OVER LOCKDOWN, BETWEEN MARCH 7TH AND JUNE 19TH

84% — WILL SMALLBONE'S PASS SUCCESS RATE – MORE ACCURATE THAN ANY OF HIS TEAMMATES

3 — ACADEMY GRADUATES WHO MADE THEIR DEBUTS: SMALLBONE, VOKINS AND TELLA

18 — POINTS WON BY SAINTS AFTER THE PL RESTART – ONLY THE MANCHESTER CLUBS (21) EARNED MORE

267 — CROSSES BY JAMES WARD-PROWSE, BEHIND ONLY ALEXANDER-ARNOLD, DE BRUYNE AND DIGNE

706 — TACKLES MADE BY SAINTS PLAYERS – ONLY LEICESTER WON THE BALL BACK MORE OFTEN

5,700,000 — VIEWERS WHO SAW SAINTS BEAT MAN CITY ON BBC – THE MOST-WATCHED PL GAME EVER

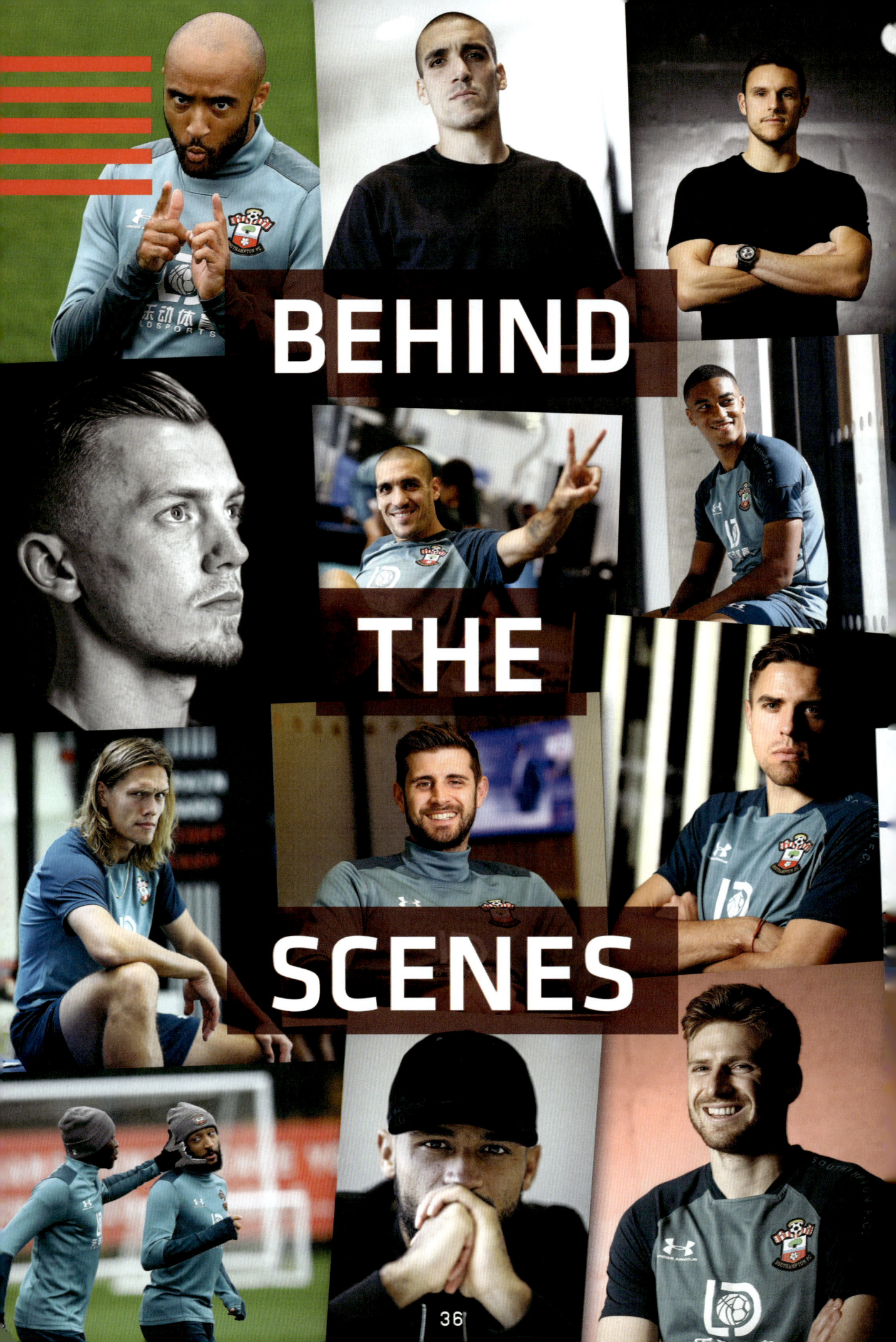

LOCKDOWN TRIVIA

2020 has been a challenging year in more ways than one! After 103 days without playing a competitive fixture, Saints finally returned to Premier League action against Norwich on June 19th. But how did the players keep themselves occupied during lockdown?

Can you match the Saints player with their lockdown activity?

Nathan Redmond	Jigsaws
Alex McCarthy	Playing guitar
Kyle Walker-Peters	Writing blogs
Jan Bednarek	Making TikToks
Shane Long	Gaming

Can you match the Saints player with this selection of songs from their lockdown playlist?

Rock 'n' Roll Star – Oasis
I Am the Resurrection – The Stone Roses
Read My Mind – The Killers

....

Come Thru – Drake
One Kiss – Calvin Harris, Dua Lipa
No Church in the Wild – Jay-Z, Kanye West

....

Sweet Caroline – Neil Diamond
Follow Me – Uncle Kracker
Circles – Post Malone

....

Viva La Vida – Coldplay
Scar Tissue – Red Hot Chili Peppers
Drops of Jupiter – Train

....

Seaside – The Kooks
Bloodstream – Ed Sheeran
Shotgun – George Ezra

....

Answers on page 62.

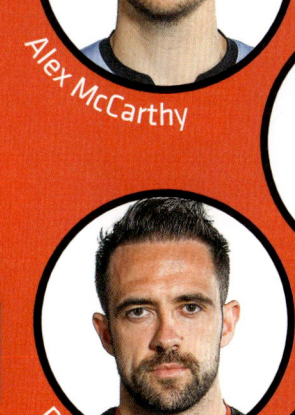

MEET THE NEXT GENERATION

Another year means more fresh talent produced by the world-famous Saints Academy! In 2019/20, WILL SMALLBONE and JAKE VOKINS sampled their first taste of life in the Premier League, before signing long-term contracts with the club…

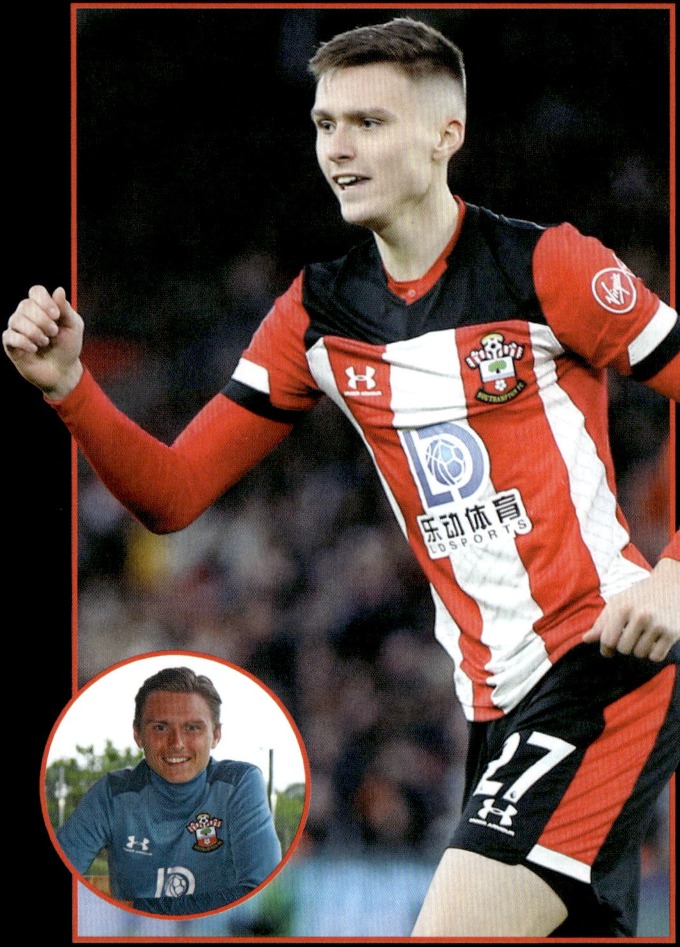

IN PROFILE

Name Will Smallbone
Position Central midfield
Date of Birth 21/02/2000
Birthplace Basingstoke
Height 173cm
Weight 61kg
Debut vs Huddersfield (H), 04/01/2020
2019/20 stats 10 apps, 1 goal
International Republic of Ireland U19

IN PROFILE

Name Jake Vokins
Position Left-back
Date of Birth 17/03/2000
Birthplace Oxford
Height 180cm
Weight 70kg
Debut vs Man City (A), 29/10/2019
2019/20 stats 3 apps, 1 goal
International England U19

What are your favourite memories of watching Saints?

WS I remember going to Wembley for the Johnstone's Paint Trophy final. I would've only been nine or 10, but that's a day I still remember fondly. I remember seeing Gareth Bale come through and how good he was – seeing what he's gone on to achieve has been special.

JV For me, as a left-back, I remember watching the likes of Gareth Bale, Luke Shaw and Matt Targett – three players who have come through the Academy that I've always looked up to and tried to learn from.

How did progressing through the Academy prepare you for life in the first team?

WS As a youngster growing up, you see the players coming through and making their debuts and it gives you that drive and hunger. You know that if you're good enough, one day you will get the chance to play.

JV I got scouted when I was six and I've been training with the club ever since, so it's 14 years that I've been involved with Southampton. They don't just concentrate on making good players, they concentrate on making good human beings as well. They just want us to develop into the best person and best player that we can.

How did it feel to make your first-team debut?

WS When you're actually involved you get so wrapped up in it, and it's only when you get time to sit back and think about it that it properly sinks in. It was weird for Jake and I to both make our debuts and both to score in the same game, but it was special for us and for the Academy.

JV It may not have been a long amount of time, but to get on the pitch and make my debut against Man City was unreal. It's something I'd worked hard for, so it was a special moment for me and my family. I'll never forget the day against Huddersfield – making my full starting debut – and to top it off with a win and a goal… I couldn't have been happier.

Which of the first-team players has had the biggest influence on you?

WS Prowsey (James Ward-Prowse) has been great – obviously he plays in the same position as me and he's come through the Academy as well, so he's been a big help. Jack Stephens has been good to me as well – they've both been in my shoes at one point, and I think they understand what they needed at that time to help them settle in.

JV Ryan Bertrand has definitely helped me a lot. We chat loads during training, and after the sessions he's always giving me tips on what I can do to be the best full-back I can be. It's crazy that I was cleaning his boots and now I'm training alongside him every day!

What are you hoping to achieve in the future?

WS In a perfect world, I just want to play as many games as I can and help the club get back into the top half of the table, fighting for European places.

JV I just want to make more appearances and prove to the manager that he can trust me. It's important I take the opportunities when they come, keep developing as a player and keep improving.

SOUTHAMPTON FC WOMEN

Another dominant league season for Southampton FC Women was cruelly cut short by coronavirus, meaning the team were unable to secure promotion – but that's not to say there were not plenty of memorable moments in 2019/20...

Saints kicked off their FA Women's National League campaign with a 5-2 victory over Chesham United, before a run of seven successive clean sheets saw them take the division by storm.

Just before the Christmas break, Saints' young squad showed their spirit to upset higher league opposition in the FA Cup second round, overcoming Yeovil away from home in a dramatic penalty shoot-out.

Marieanne Spacey-Cale's charges repeated the feat in the third round by ousting Cardiff, bouncing back after conceding an early goal to progress 2-1 in south Wales.

The impact of the fourth-round meeting with Coventry United exceeded all expectations, as a record-breaking 4,510 spectators were in attendance at St Mary's as part of an historic FA Cup double-header weekend.

"We cannot allow the disappointing decision to null and void the season to detract from the brilliant progress this club has made both on and off the pitch. The Women's programme has developed through the support of the club and we will continue to strive to be the very best we can."

Marieanne Spacey-Cale, Head of Girls' and Women's Football

Although the result did not go Saints' way, as the Championship visitors ran out 4-1 winners, it was still an experience to savour and showcased how far the women's and girls' programme has come in the last two years, providing a platform for young aspiring players.

Saints bounced back to book their place in the Hampshire Cup final and remained unbeaten in the league, while local rivals Portsmouth were defeated in the quarter-finals of the League Cup, only for a solitary set-piece goal to end the team's hopes of reaching another final, as Championship hosts Sunderland advanced.

Nobody could have foreseen that the resounding 7-0 victory over Maidenhead at the start of March would bring down the curtain on the season, but The FA announced some weeks later to null and void all women's leagues from Tier 3 down, leaving Saints needing to repeat their heroics in 2020/21.

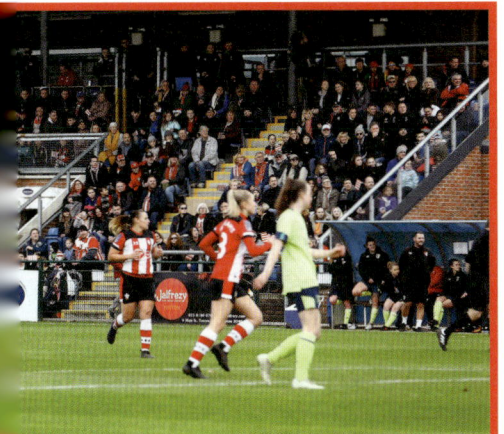

BEST OF THE SAINTS

We've been catching up with some proper Saints legends to find out their favourite memories of pulling on the famous red and white stripes!

BEST GAME?

DW Scoring my first hat-trick against Coventry in the 8-2 win towards the end of the 1983/84 season. Steve Moran also hit a hat-trick, but he'd scored a couple before, so when we went into the dressing room all the players said I should have the matchball!

MLT We played Liverpool in October 1989, they were unbeaten in the league coming to The Dell and we ended up beating them 4-1. We were very positive – we played 4-2-4 and absolutely smashed them. It could've been 8-1!

CL The last game at The Dell. It was a fairy-tale ending. Me and Matthew Le Tissier were really close at the time and I had a bet with him; if he won the game for us, I would buy him a case of Malibu and coke! It couldn't have ended in a better way than with the legend himself scoring the last winning goal.

RL There are three that come straight into my head; the Coventry and Plymouth games, because they were the two promotions, and the Man City one, because we were all playing in our first Premier League game and I scored my first Premier League goal.

DANNY WALLACE
1980-1989   Apps 317   Goals 79

BEST TEAMMATE?

DW These players made a few goals for me, so I would say Jimmy Case and Steve Williams. Jimmy was incredible – a great passer of the ball and I loved the way we gelled on the pitch. I could just flick my head and he'd know I'd be running, and put the ball right in front of me.

MLT Ronnie Ekelund in the 1994/95 season, when Bally (Alan Ball) brought him over on loan from Barcelona. That experience for me, playing alongside him, was just amazing. We were on the same wavelength from the first training session we had together.

CL Matthew Le Tissier was the most gifted – he was special. As a finisher, he was world class. I had heard about him, but to be honest I knew very little about Southampton before I came. I was only there for two or three days before I made my debut!

RL Adam Lallana. I think being in League One helped him, because he was playing week in week out, getting stronger and tougher. When he got to the Championship, he was still growing and still maturing, but when he got to the Premier League he was unbelievable.

MATT LE TISSIER
1986-2002   Apps 540   Goals 209

CLAUS LUNDEKVAM
1996-2007   Apps 413   Goals 2

BEST OPPONENT?

DW Paul Parker, who later became a teammate at Manchester United. His pace was on a par with mine, so we had some good battles. He later became a friend, but it was always good to pit our skills against each other.

MLT Thierry Henry. He came in 1999, and I was playing in the game when he scored his first Arsenal goal. Sometimes he was like a man playing in boys' football – he was that good. It was like he floated on the air without even touching the ground.

CL I feel blessed to have played against so many world-class strikers, but my answer to this question has always been Thierry Henry. To play against a striker who was so quick but so clever, with his abilities... he was probably the one I struggled with the most.

RL David Silva. You can normally stop most players, by man marking them or putting two men on them, but no matter what we seemed to do with Silva, he would just calm it down, get Man City playing and get them out of situations. He was devastating, and still is today.

BEST MANAGER?

DW Lawrie McMenemy and Sir Alex Ferguson were very similar characters. I was at Southampton for nine years and Lawrie was brilliant with me as a manager – just a really lovely person. Sir Alex was the same, you could speak to him about anything.

MLT Alan Ball. He just said to me, 'do what you're good at. Don't bother defending, because we know you're rubbish at that, but when we are defending, get yourself in a position where, when we get the ball, we can pass to you'. He just played to my strengths.

CL The best years were under Gordon Strachan. He was really clear. Tough, but honest and fair. We hated him for the first few months he was there, because the training was so hard! He ran us senseless for the first few months, but after a while we saw the benefits of it.

RL The three best managers I had in my career were the ones at Southampton, but the best one was Mauricio Pochettino. On the pitch, technically, he had a different way to look at it, and learning from him was one of the best things I've ever done in football.

RICKIE LAMBERT
2009-2014   Apps 235   Goals 117

CULT HERO: GULY DO PRADO

There's always been something unique about Brazilian football, and GULY DO PRADO still stands alone as Southampton's original Samba star. We put 10 questions to our former No 10, who helped the club win back-to-back promotions to the Premier League, capturing the hearts of thousands of Saints fans along the way...

FACTFILE

Name: Guly do Prado
Date of Birth: 31/12/1981
Nationality: Brazilian
Birthplace: Campinas, State of São Paulo
Position: Forward
Joined Saints: 2010
Signed From: Cesena, Italy
Left Saints: 2014
Apps: 118
Goals: 23

You first signed for Southampton on loan in 2010. How did the move come about?

I was tired of Italy, so I called my agent to look for something new. That's what happened, and we found Southampton's door was open. I'm very thankful to Nicola Cortese for that.

What were your first impressions of Southampton, of English football and English culture?

Everything was very well organised, with crowded stadiums – even in the middle of the week! I found it incredible. I was happy with the culture and I learned a lot from the English people. I miss it.

Did you believe it was possible for the club to rise from League One to the Premier League in two seasons?

Yes, I felt it because our team was very good and superior to the others, with all respect to them.

You quickly developed a special connection with the Southampton fans. How do you remember them?

I was happy with the Saints fans at all times, but especially when we won the Coventry away game (4-2 in the Championship). Away from home it was a very difficult game, and then hearing the crowd shouting my name was remarkable for me – not to mention the invasion of the field at the first promotion, which was wonderful.

Which of your Southampton teammates helped you the most, and who are you still in contact with?

Morgan Schneiderlin and José Fonte – these two were important to me and I always talk to them when I can.

Who were the best players you played with and against in England?

The best players I played with in England were Adam Lallana and Morgan – I learned a lot from them. The best I played against was David Silva.

Your spectacular goals against Blackpool and Bristol Rovers are still fondly remembered, as well as your pre-season hat-trick! What is your favourite Guly moment at Southampton?

My happy moments are every day of my life because people stop me to ask about Southampton. People look at me and see Southampton.

You left Southampton in 2014. How has your life changed over the last six years?

For the first two months it was difficult to accept I had left Southampton, to be honest. But after that my life started to change and I am so happy for what has happened in those years. I'm proud about that.

Are you still playing football, and what do you hope to do when you retire?

I stopped my career a few months ago – now I work with the kids.

What are your passions away from football?

I enjoy spending time with my family, playing football with my friends and having barbecues.

CREATE YOUR OWN SAINTS CULT HERO XI!

WORD PUZZLES

WORDSEARCH

- Away Win
- Mary Saint
- Premier League
- Red and White
- Sammy Saint
- Sash
- Southampton
- South Coast Derby
- St Mary's
- Team Talk
- Under Armour
- We March On

CODEBREAKER

Can you unlock the code? Answer all 10 questions correctly to reveal the bonus answer!

1. Who scored Saints' first and last goals of 2019/20?
2. Josh Sims spent time on loan representing the Red Bulls in which city?
3. Who is the only player to have scored more free-kicks for Saints than James Ward-Prowse in the Premier League era?
4. Mohamed Salisu joined Saints from which Spanish club?
5. Ex-Saints brothers Danny, Rodney and Ray share which surname?
6. Before 2020/21, who was the last player to score a Premier League hat-trick for Saints?
7. Saints thrashed Portsmouth 4-0 in which competition?
8. Danny Ings began his professional career at which club?
9. Who was the only player to score on his Saints debut in 2019/20?
10. Who made his Saints debut as a late substitute against Norwich in the first game after lockdown?

Answers on page 62.

CHEF'S CORNER

Saints' Executive Head Chef, Zoltan Szalas, shares some more of his favourite recipes for you to try out at home...

DRINK LIKE A SAINT! INCREDIBLE HULK SMOOTHIE

When you see the colour of this, you'll understand the name!

FACT: Packed full of nutrition, it provides a nice boost for your immune system, containing a wide variety of vitamins, including A, B6, B9, C, K1, iron, calcium, folic acid and magnesium!

Serves: 2

Ingredients

- 1 handful of spinach, washed and chopped
- 1 handful of curly kale, washed and chopped
- 350ml of almond or oat milk (can be replaced with cow's milk if you prefer)
- 140g diced mango, either fresh or frozen
- 140g diced pineapple, either fresh or frozen
- 1/5 a teaspoon (2.5g) grated root ginger
- ½ lemon, juiced

Method

1. Add the spinach and kale with the milk into a blender.
2. Peel and grate the root ginger, then add into the blender with the rest of the fruits. If the milk isn't cold enough, you can add a couple of ice cubes to chill it.
3. Blitz until smooth.

DRINK LIKE A SAINT! FUNKY FRUIT SMOOTHIE

A simple recipe but packed with flavour and great for a daily vitamin boost!

Serves: 2

Ingredients

- 1 carrot, peeled and chopped
- 1cm root ginger, peeled and finely chopped
- 1 orange, peeled
- 1 apple, cored and chopped
- 200ml water

Method

Place all of the ingredients in a blender and blitz for one minute, or until smooth. Easy as that!

GETTING TO KNOW… KYLE WALKER-PETERS

Saints' first signing of the summer was a familiar face, as KYLE WALKER-PETERS put pen to paper on a five-year deal at St Mary's following a successful loan spell…

Why did you choose to join Southampton in January, initially on loan?

When I spoke to the manager, he made it clear to me that he knew what type of player I was and he knew that the team's style suited the way I like to play. When I watched Southampton games, I did get that feeling, so it ended up being quite an easy decision in terms of how to develop myself playing in a style and system that I like.

Did you know any of the players before you signed?

I did! I knew Gunny (Angus Gunn) and Josh Sims from England youth teams, and I'd met Redders (Nathan Redmond), Ryan Bertrand and Michael Obafemi, so it was easy settling in.

What do you consider your greatest strengths as a player?

I think technically I'm good and I enjoy defending one against one, but my main asset is my energy – I'm always running around, never strolling, and I think that's important. This team plays with high intensity, high energy pressing, and that's what I like to do.

What areas of your own game do you most want to learn and improve?

I'd say maybe my end product. My assist record at Tottenham wasn't too bad, but a lot of times I get into good areas and sometimes I think I could do better with my final ball.

What has been the best moment of your career so far?

I'd probably say my game on Boxing Day in 2018 against Bournemouth, when I registered three assists. I couldn't actually believe it – I remember after the third one saying to Christian Eriksen, 'I don't know what's happening, this is crazy!'

What is your favourite thing to do outside of football?

I do play a lot of PlayStation. I always love to compete, which probably isn't great because you need to give your mind a rest. I play a lot of NBA with Dominic Solanke and Dele Alli – I just like to chill and spend time with my friends.

QUICK-FIRE QUESTIONS

Who was your favourite player growing up?

I would say Ronaldinho. I loved that he was always smiling on the pitch, and obviously how talented he was with his skills, goals and assists.

Who is your favourite full-back of all time?

I love Dani Alves – I always watched him for Barcelona. He's the most decorated footballer of all time, so for him to be a right-back is pretty cool.

Who is your sporting hero?

Outside of football, I like Usain Bolt. I think he inspired everyone with the way he conducted himself before his races – always cool and a bit different. I really like Roger Federer as well; another cool guy who never looks fazed – he could be having the worst game and you would never know.

Can you play any other sports?

I like basketball, but I wouldn't say I can play it because I'm too small! I'd love to have a basketball court in my garden and shoot hoops with my mates.

Who are the best players you've played with and against?

I've played against some good players, like Thiago and Coutinho at Bayern and Barcelona. I think as Messi came on, I came off! I've played against Cristiano Ronaldo as well. The best I've played with... Harry Kane. He's ridiculous.

Who is the most famous person you've ever met?

I've met David Beckham, Neymar and Kobe Bryant, so it would have to be one of those.

How would you describe your personality?

Quite bubbly – I get on with everyone. If I have an argument with someone on the pitch, that's it, it's forgotten. I'm not someone who can stay angry for long. I like to think I'm quite a fun person!

IN PROFILE

Name	Kyle Walker-Peters
Date of Birth	13/04/1997
Birthplace	Edmonton, north London
Height	173cm
Weight	62kg
Contract	2025
Signed from	Tottenham
Tottenham stats	24 apps, 1 goal
Saints loan stats	10 apps, 0 goals
England U21 stats	9 apps, 0 goals

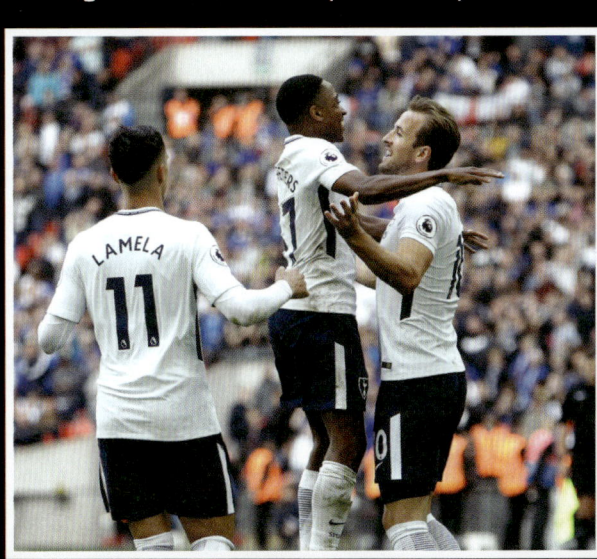

2020/21 KIT

AWAY

With a sleek navy blue design, the 2020/21 away kit harks back to the colour used for the team's shorts and socks throughout much of its early history, from 1891 through to 1950

The colour is complemented by accents of yellow and solent blue that conjure memories of the iconic 1976 FA Cup final victory

Solent blue is the primary colour of both the shorts and socks – the latter featuring a navy stripe with yellow detail for a striking combination

THIRD

The white 2020/21 third shirt boasts a red sash across the left shoulder, in contrast to the home shirt

The all-white strip features red detail on the shorts and socks

The design conjures fond memories of Saints' 2010/11 League One promotion-winning kit

HOME

The 2020/21 home strip is a modern twist on the club's iconic sash kit first worn back in 1885

The 135th anniversary kit features a predominantly red shirt with a white sash over the right shoulder

The black and white trim around the neckline and sleeves is complemented by black shorts and red socks, which feature a single white stripe across the middle

GK

The home and away 2020/21 goalkeeper shirts are yellow and pink respectively, ensuring our last line of defence really stand out from the crowd!

THE SASH IS BACK!

THINK YOU COULD DO BETTER? DESIGN YOUR OWN!

23 DAYS LATER...

The shortest off-season ever? Just 23 days after finally completing their 2019/20 Premier League campaign, Saints were back to work and preparing for the new season.

MEET THE OPPOSITION

ARSENAL

Nickname: The Gunners
Ground: Emirates Stadium
Capacity: 60,704
Manager: Mikel Arteta
Last season: 8th
Top scorer: Pierre-Emerick Aubameyang, 29 goals
Key player: Nicolas Pépé

Success would be...
Following FA Cup success and a strong end to last term under new boss Arteta, the Gunners will be targeting the top four.

ASTON VILLA

Nickname: The Villans
Ground: Villa Park
Capacity: 42,095
Manager: Dean Smith
Last season: 17th
Top scorer: Jack Grealish, 10 goals
Key player: Jack Grealish

Success would be...
After escaping the drop on the final day, Villa will be hoping for a less stressful campaign, but a relegation battle is likely.

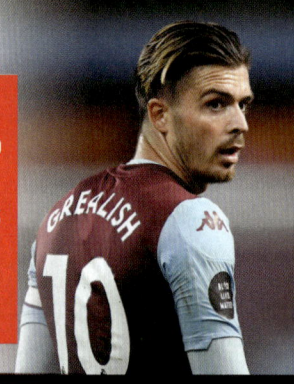

BRIGHTON & HOVE ALBION

Nickname: The Seagulls
Ground: Amex Stadium
Capacity: 30,750
Manager: Graham Potter
Last season: 15th
Top scorer: Neal Maupay, 10 goals
Key player: Dan Burn

Success would be...
Potter introduced a new playing style and after a brush with relegation will want his side to push on towards mid-table.

BURNLEY

Nickname: The Clarets
Ground: Turf Moor
Capacity: 21,944
Manager: Sean Dyche
Last season: 10th
Top scorer: Chris Wood, 14 goals
Key player: James Tarkowski

Success would be...
If they can strengthen their squad over the summer, the Clarets could be in with a strong shout of a Europa League spot.

CHELSEA

Nickname: The Blues
Ground: Stamford Bridge
Capacity: 40,834
Manager: Frank Lampard
Last season: 4th
Top scorer: Tammy Abraham, 17 goals
Key player: Timo Werner

Success would be...
With big money to spend, the Blues will be eyeing a title challenge, the last eight of the Champions League and silverware.

CRYSTAL PALACE

Nickname: The Eagles
Ground: Selhurst Park
Capacity: 25,486
Manager: Roy Hodgson
Last season: 14th
Top scorer: Jordan Ayew, 9 goals
Key player: Wilfried Zaha

Success would be...
Keeping the mercurial Zaha and bolstering an ageing side will be key to Hodgson's men avoiding another lower-half finish.

EVERTON

Nickname: The Toffees
Ground: Goodison Park
Capacity: 39,414
Manager: Carlo Ancelotti
Last season: 12th
Top scorer: Dominic Calvert-Lewin & Richarlison, 13 goals each
Key player: Richarlison

Success would be...
After their lowest finish for 16 years, Ancelotti will be backed in the transfer market and expect a top-six push.

FULHAM

Nickname: The Cottagers
Ground: Craven Cottage
Capacity: 19,000
Manager: Scott Parker
Last season: 4th (Championship, promoted via play-offs)
Top scorer: Aleksandar Mitrović, 26 goals
Key player: Tom Cairney

Success would be...
Avoiding the transfer mistakes of their last stint in the top flight and staying clear of trouble would be a job well done.

LEEDS UNITED

Nickname: The Whites
Ground: Elland Road
Capacity: 37,890
Manager: Marcelo Bielsa
Last season: 1st (Championship)
Top scorer: Patrick Bamford, 16 goals
Key player: Kalvin Phillips

Success would be...
Remaining in the Premier League after a 16-year absence, although a talented squad could be capable of surprising teams.

LEICESTER CITY

Nickname: The Foxes
Ground: King Power Stadium
Capacity: 32,261
Manager: Brendan Rodgers
Last season: 5th
Top scorer: Jamie Vardy, 23 goals
Key player: James Maddison

Success would be...
After slipping out of the top four on the final day, Rodgers will have designs on cementing a Champions League place.

LIVERPOOL

Nickname: The Reds
Ground: Anfield
Capacity: 53,394
Manager: Jürgen Klopp
Last season: 1st
Top scorer: Mohamed Salah, 23 goals
Key player: Sadio Mané

Success would be...
Having ended their 30-year long wait to be crowned champions of England, the Reds will be bidding to retain their title.

MANCHESTER CITY

Nickname: The Citizens
Ground: Etihad Stadium
Capacity: 55,017
Manager: Pep Guardiola
Last season: 2nd
Top scorer: Raheem Sterling, 30 goals
Key player: Kevin De Bruyne

Success would be...
Losing their grip on the Premier League trophy hurt and City will be desperate to win it back as well as conquer Europe.

MANCHESTER UNITED

Nickname: The Red Devils
Ground: Old Trafford
Capacity: 74,879
Manager: Ole Gunnar Solskjaer
Last season: 3rd
Top scorer: Anthony Martial, 23 goals
Key player: Marcus Rashford

Success would be...
Continued progression under Solskjaer will require significant investment if United are to bring back the glory days.

NEWCASTLE UNITED

Nickname: The Magpies
Ground: St James' Park
Capacity: 52,305
Manager: Steve Bruce
Last season: 13th
Top scorer: Jonjo Shelvey, 6 goals
Key player: Allan Saint-Maximin

Success would be...
Among the lowest scorers in the league last season, Newcastle can push up the table if they can hit the net more regularly.

SHEFFIELD UNITED

Nickname: The Blades
Ground: Bramall Lane
Capacity: 32,125
Manager: Chris Wilder
Last season: 9th
Top scorer: Lys Mousset and Oliver McBurnie, 6 goals each
Key player: Chris Basham

Success would be...
The Blades took the Premier League by storm on their return to the top flight but 'second-season syndrome' is a concern.

TOTTENHAM HOTSPUR

Nickname: Spurs
Ground: Tottenham Hotspur Stadium
Capacity: 62,303
Manager: Jose Mourinho
Last season: 6th
Top scorer: Harry Kane, 24 goals
Key player: Son Heung-Min

Success would be...
A return to the top four places and a domestic trophy would surely please even the most pessimistic Tottenham fan.

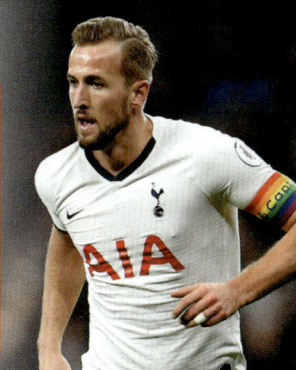

WEST BROMWICH ALBION

Nickname: The Baggies
Ground: The Hawthorns
Capacity: 26,850
Manager: Slaven Bilić
Last season: 2nd (Championship)
Top scorer: Charlie Austin, 10 goals
Key player: Matheus Pereira

Success would be...
Something of a yo-yo club down the years, West Brom would happily settle for 17th spot and a chance to consolidate.

WEST HAM UNITED

Nickname: The Hammers
Ground: London Stadium
Capacity: 60,000
Manager: David Moyes
Last season: 16th
Top scorer: Michail Antonio, 10 goals
Key player: Declan Rice

Success would be...
After a worrying brush with relegation last term, Moyes will be looking to push his side into the top half of the table.

WOLVERHAMPTON WANDERERS

Nickname: Wolves
Ground: Molineux
Capacity: 32,050
Manager: Nuno Espírito Santo
Last season: 7th
Top scorer: Raúl Jiménez, 20 goals
Key player: Adama Traoré

Success would be...
After two seventh-place finishes, can Wolves go one better? With some talented players, you wouldn't bet against it.

THANK YOU!

"One thing the Premier League restart proved to us is that football is not quite the same without fans inside the stadium." - Ralph Hasenhüttl

QUIZ ANSWERS

Pages 24-25: QUIZ OF THE SEASON

1. Standard Liège
2. Brighton & Hove Albion
3. Michael Obafemi
4. Nathan Redmond
5. West Ham United
6. Watford and Norwich City
7. Jake Vokins and Will Smallbone
8. Crystal Palace
9. 9th
10. Sofiane Boufal
11. Aston Villa
12. James Ward-Prowse
13. Kevin Danso, Ryan Bertrand, Moussa Djenepo and Jack Stephens
14. Ché Adams
15. Arsenal
16. 26
17. Michael Obafemi
18. Three
19. Bournemouth
20. James Beattie

Page 39: LOCKDOWN TRIVIA

1. Match the lockdown activities

Nathan Redmond	Making TikToks
Alex McCarthy	Writing blogs
Kyle Walker-Peters	Gaming
Jan Bednarek	Jigsaws
Shane Long	Playing guitar

2. Match the lockdown playlists

JACK STEPHENS
Rock 'n' Roll Star – Oasis
I Am the Resurrection – The Stone Roses
Read My Mind – The Killers

JAMES WARD-PROWSE
Come Thru – Drake
One Kiss – Calvin Harris, Dua Lipa
No Church in the Wild – Jay-Z, Kanye West

ANGUS GUNN
Sweet Caroline – Neil Diamond
Follow Me – Uncle Kracker
Circles – Post Malone

SHANE LONG
Viva La Vida – Coldplay
Scar Tissue – Red Hot Chili Peppers
Drops of Jupiter – Train

DANNY INGS
Seaside – The Kooks
Bloodstream – Ed Sheeran
Shotgun – George Ezra

Page 48: WORDSEARCH

Page 48: CODEBREAKER

INGS
NEWYORK
LETISSIER
VALLADOLID
WALLACE
MANE
CARABAOCUP
BOURNEMOUTH
SMALLBONE
TELLA